THE MEANING OF
meow

365 SMILES
FOR CAT LOVERS

new seasons®

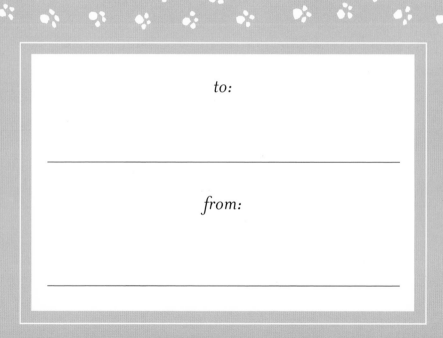

Original inspirations written by
Charles Dowdy, T.J. Dugan and Kelly Womer

january 1

One of the most striking differences
between a cat and a lie is that a
cat has only nine lives.

—Mark Twain

notes

What's up?

anniversary gifts

	traditional	modern		traditional	modern
first	paper	clock	thirteenth	lace	textiles & furs
second	cotton	china	fourteenth	ivory	gold jewelry
third	leather	crystal & glass	fifteenth	crystal	watch
fourth	fruit & flowers	appliances	twentieth	china	platinum
fifth	woodenware	silverware	twenty-fifth	silver	silver
sixth	candy & iron	woodenware	thirtieth	pearls	diamond jewelry
seventh	wool & copper	desk set	thirty-fifth	coral	jade
eighth	bronze & pottery	linen & lace	fortieth	ruby	ruby
ninth	pottery & willow	leather goods	fiftieth	gold	gold
tenth	tin & aluminum	diamond jewelry	fifty-fifth	emeralds	emeralds
eleventh	steel	jewelry	sixtieth	diamonds	diamonds
twelfth	silk & linens	pearls			

january 3

A black-and-white cat that belongs to
the Clintons, Socks, received approximately
75,000 letters and parcels each week while
in the White House. *Socks Goes to Washington*,
the First Cat's autobiography,
was published in 1993.

cat
trivia

december

birthdays & anniversaries

_____   _____

_____   _____

_____   _____

_____   _____

_____   _____

_____   _____

_____   _____

birthstone: *turquoise*
flower: *poinsettia*

january 4

1. *The Silent Miaow, A Manual for Kittens, Strays, and Homeless Cats* —Paul Gallico

2. *The Quotable Cat* —Lisa A. Rogak

3. *Old Possum's Book of Practical Cats* —T.S. Eliot

4. *In the Company of Cats - A Tribute to the Feline* —edited by Linda Sunshine

5. *My Cat's Not Fat, He's Just Big-Boned* —Nicole Hollander

6. *All I Need to Know I Learned From My Cat* —Suzy Becker

7. *Cat: Seventeenth Anniversary Edition* —B. Kliban

8. *All My Patients Are Under the Bed* —Dr. Louis J. Camuti, with Marilyn and Haskel Frankel

9. *A Cat's Little Instruction Book* —Leigh W. Rutledge

10. *Cat Hiss-Tory: A Feline Tour Through the Ages* —Frederica Templeton

top 10 cat books

november

birthdays & anniversaries

_____   _____

_____   _____

_____   _____

_____   _____

_____   _____

_____   _____

_____   _____

birthstone: *topaz*
flower: *chrysanthemum*

Little Kittens
by Louisa May Alcat

if cats could write

october

birthdays & anniversaries

_____   _____

_____   _____

_____   _____

_____   _____

_____   _____

_____   _____

_____   _____

birthstone: *opal*
flower: *dahlia*

january 6

Who me? Shed?

september
birthdays & anniversaries

_____   _____

_____   _____

_____   _____

_____   _____

_____   _____

_____   _____

_____   _____

birthstone: *sapphire*
flower: *aster*

january 7

Abraham Lincoln was a cat lover. He had
four cats while living in the White House.
His cat, Tabby, was the first White House cat.

august

birthdays & anniversaries

_____   _____

_____   _____

_____   _____

_____   _____

_____   _____

_____   _____

_____   _____

birthstone: *peridot*

flower: *gladiolus*

The more people I meet,
the more I like my cat.

—Anonymous

july
birthdays & anniversaries

_____   _____

_____   _____

_____   _____

_____   _____

_____   _____

_____   _____

_____   _____

birthstone: *ruby*
flower: *sweet pea*

january 9

You know what they say about curiosity…
Here's hoping there's safety in numbers.

june
birthdays & anniversaries

_____   _____

_____   _____

_____   _____

_____   _____

_____   _____

_____   _____

_____   _____

birthstone: *pearl*
flower: *rose*

january 10

In ancient Egypt a
person could receive the
death penalty for killing a cat.

may
birthdays & anniversaries

_____   _____

_____   _____

_____   _____

_____   _____

_____   _____

_____   _____

_____   _____

birthstone: *emerald*
flower: *lily of the valley*

What's the best bone
to feed a dog?

(A trombone.)

april
birthdays & anniversaries

_____   _____

_____   _____

_____   _____

_____   _____

_____   _____

_____   _____

_____   _____

birthstone: *diamond*
flower: *daisy or lily*

cat•a•log [ka-te-log] n.
something good to hide behind when
a cat doesn't want to be seen.

 cat vocabulary

march

birthdays & anniversaries

_____	_____
_____	_____
_____	_____
_____	_____
_____	_____
_____	_____
_____	_____

birthstone: *aquamarine*
flower: *violet*

january 13

The humans have finally
accepted my proper
place on the pedestal.

february

birthdays & anniversaries

_____   _____

_____   _____

_____   _____

_____   _____

_____   _____

_____   _____

_____   _____

birthstone: *amethyst*

flower: *primrose*

january 14

Famous expatriate author
Ernest Hemingway had 30 pet cats.

january

birthdays & anniversaries

_____   _____

_____   _____

_____   _____

_____   _____

_____   _____

_____   _____

_____   _____

birthstone: *garnet*

flower: *carnation*

The smallest feline is a masterpiece.

—Leonardo da Vinci

I never met a kitten
I didn't like.

january 16

That's right, pal.
Step away from the catnip.

december 30

No matter how much cats fight,
there always seem to be plenty of kittens.

—Abraham Lincoln

january 17

Misty Malarky Ying Yang was a Siamese cat that belonged to President Carter's daughter, Amy. He was First Cat from 1977 to 1981.

When I play with my cat,
who knows if I am not a pastime
for her more than she is to me?

—Michel de Montaigne

january 18

I won't tell
if you won't tell.

december 28

You put your left foot in,
you take your left foot out…

january 19

Reach an agreement with someone in
your neighborhood so they will check on
your animals when you aren't home.
Agree to do the same for them.

december 27

Calvin, a Maltese stray who took over
Harriet Beecher Stowe's house,
reportedly sat on Stowe's
shoulders while she wrote.

cat
trivia

Aquarius

Just as the caterpillar has to cocoon before becoming a butterfly, you, too, have spent more than your fair share of time out of sight. Your time of reemergence is nigh. Come out of the top of the closet, from behind the curtains, from under the couch. Show yourself and enjoy a sociable reward for your efforts. By all means stay out of car engines this winter, no matter how warm they might be.

december 26

cat•e•la•tion
[kat-ee-lay-shun] n.
the feeling that arrives when
the supper dish is filled

 cat vocabulary

january 21

Beerbohm, a tabby, was London's
longest-serving theater mouser.
Beerbohm served at the Globe Theater
from the mid-70s to 1995.

december 25

The heaviest domestic cat in recorded history, Himmy, was a tabby that weighed 46 pounds, 15.25 oz.

january 22

A kitten is life's way of telling
you to always enjoy the simplest
pleasures to their fullest.

december 24

Don't try to play
cute with me, mister.
I saw you out with the dog.

january 23

Dog shmog.

Cats are a mysterious kind of folk.
There is more passing in their
minds than we are aware of.

—Sir Walter Scott

The record for most kittens in a lifetime is held by Dusty. She gave birth to 420 kittens.

cat
trivia

Capricorn

This will be a wonderful time for you on the financial front, Capricorn. All that hard work your owner has been putting in at the office might pay off. It may be the lottery or an inheritance, but you are coming into the money. No more cheap food. Fresh litter twice a day. And no going to the vet when she travels…you're going, too. All nine of your lives are looking up.

cat•a•lyst
[ka-te-lest] *n.*
designation given to the upper echelon
of cat stars such as Heathcliff and Garfield.
Generally these are thought of as pets that
can green light their own projects.

 cat vocabulary

december 21

I'm too sexy for my collar.

There is nothing sweeter than his peace
when at rest, for there is nothing brisker
than his life when in motion.

—Christopher Smart

French emperor Napoleon Bonaparte
was afflicted with Ailurophobia,
or the fear of cats.

I plead the fifth.

If animals could speak the dog would
be a blundering outspoken fellow,
but the cat would have the rare grace
of never saying a word too much.

—Mark Twain

Composer Henri Sauguet's cat, Cody,
was claimed to be fond of Claude Debussy
compositions. The cat became ecstatic when
Debussy songs were played on the piano.

cat
trivia

december 18

A black-and-white cat named
Humphrey was a longtime mascot of
the Prime Minister's residence in London.

I'm going to close my eyes, and when I open them there'd better be a squeaky toy in front of me.

One should be just as careful in choosing one's
pleasures as in avoiding calamities.

—Chinese proverb

january 30

It's very hard to be
polite if you're a cat.

—Anonymous

december 16

Have good pictures of
your cat on hand in case
your pet turns up missing.
You can use the pictures
to help locate your pet.

cat
tips

Forget chicken soup—kittens
are good for the soul.

december 15

Edgar Allen Poe took his cat, Catarina, everywhere he went. She frequently sat on his shoulder as he wrote, and inspired *The Black Cat*.

cat trivia

I am as vigilant as a
cat to steal cream.

—William Shakespeare

Dog food?
You let me eat dog food?
I think I'm gonna bark!

A Tail of Two Kitties
by Charles Kittens

if cats could write

cat•e•bul•i•ence
[kat-ee-bul-yents] *n.*
the feeling a cat has when he
finds himself with bird in mouth.

 cat vocabulary

Reach for the moth,
but keep one paw
on the ground.

december 12

Did you hear about the
dog who thought he
was a werewolf?

(He's better nooooooow!)

Famed English author Thomas Hardy
had a Blue Persian named Cobby
that was given to him late in life.
Cobby vanished after Hardy died in 1928.

Heathcliff, an animated rival of Garfield,
was named after a character
in *Wuthering Heights*.

cat
trivia

1. *Cats!* - the musical

2. *That Darn Cat!*

3. *The Adventures of Milo and Otis*

4. *Dr. Seuss' The Cat in the Hat*

5. *Felix the Cat*

6. *The Aristocats*

7. *Tom and Jerry*

8. *Born Free*

9. *Cats - Caressing the Tiger*

10. *Cats and Dogs*

top 10 cat movies

december 10

It's in the genes, sweetheart.

I don't think this new diet is working for me.

Nine lives each cat may surely measure;
May yours be nine times filled with pleasure.

—Unknown

Ernest Hemingway trusted his cat
Mr. Feather Puss so much he allowed
the cat to babysit his child.

december 8

Hamlet, a white cat with gray
patches and a tabby tail, was the title
character of Val Schaffner's *Algonquin Cat*.
Hamlet was also the mascot of the
Algonquin Hotel in Manhattan.

cat
trivia

In ancient times cats
were worshiped as gods;
they have never forgotten this.

—Unknown

The only thing better than a good stretch?
A good stretch in your sleep.

cat•a•ma•ran
[ka-te-me-ran] *n.*
derogatory term for a cat
who is not that smart.

cat vocabulary

The Great Catsby
by F. Cat Fitzgerald

if cats could write

You just go ahead and continue
thinking you're in charge.

december 5

1. Acetaminophen
2. Dye
3. Laxatives
4. Rat poison
5. Antifreeze
6. Deodorant
7. Mothballs
8. Suntan lotion
9. Shoe polish
10. Poinsettia

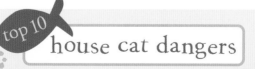

top 10 house cat dangers

Felix the Cat was the first
animated character to be the
subject of a marketing campaign.

december 4

Nelson, another of Winston Churchill's cats,
sat in a chair next to the Prime Minister
in both the Cabinet and dining rooms.
Nelson was named after Lord Nelson,
but wasn't nearly as brave.

cat
trivia

What happens when a
Dalmatian takes a shower?

(He's becomes spotless.)

I do love you;
I'm just not ready to
announce it to the world.

I said you could pet me,
but I warned you about
picking me up.

There are many intelligent
species in the universe.
They are all owned by cats.

—Anonymous

The word *grimalkin*, which is defined as
"a domestic cat; esp. an old female cat,"
originally appeared as the name of the first
witch's familiar in Shakespeare's *MacBeth*.

cat
trivia

december 1

Hodge was Dr. Samuel Johnson's favorite cat.
Johnson bought fresh oysters each
day to feed his pampered pet.

cat trivia

Know where the animal shelters
are in your area. Cats love to roam.

Cats love to
sleep softly.

-Theocritus

february 16

And this is my
"I'm just a silly little kitty"
look I give them when
I've done something
really bad.

A kitten provides the
perfect combination of
companionship and amusement.

I know you see
me sitting here.
Now pet me before
I get moody!

november 28

If you want to know
the character of a man,
find out what his cat
thinks of him.

—Anonymous

february 18

The staff of the Savoy Hotel in London places a wooden cat named Kasper at tables to avoid seating unlucky parties of 13.

november 27

Teddy Roosevelt had a variety of pets
during his stay in the White House.
One was a gray tabby named Slippers
who had six toes on each foot.

cat
trivia

Pisces

The world is leaving you behind, Pisces. Sleep and tuna are not the only things life has to offer. Is it that you are bored? Perhaps you should get back into your traditional profession of pest removal. Otherwise, at least go outside and get some fresh air. Give your human some space; your relationship will be stronger for it.

Just so you know, one more stunt like that
and it's good-bye houseplants.

I coined the phrase,
"sitting pretty."

cat•ec•sta•sy
[kat-ek-stah-see] n.
a cat's state of being during laptime

 cat vocabulary

february 21

Morris, of 9 Lives fame, was originally called Lucky because he was rescued from an animal shelter near Chicago.

cat trivia

Sizi lived with humanitarian
Albert Schweitzer at his clinic
in Africa. Although Schweitzer
was left-handed, he would write
prescriptions with his right hand
if Sizi was sleeping on his left arm.

cat
trivia

A kitten is so flexible that she is
almost double; the hind parts are
equivalent to another kitten with which
the forepart plays. She does not
discover that her tail belongs to
her until you tread on it.

—Henry David Thoreau

A house without either
a cat or a dog is the
house of a scoundrel.

—Portuguese proverb

A cat sees us as the dogs.
A cat sees himself as the human.

—Unknown

Sagittarius

Health will be something you must watch. Have you been a spendthrift with your lives or using them judiciously? Well, this would be a good time for you to lie low. There have been helping hands to get you out of trees the last few months. But you can't expect that help will always be around the corner.

I may have fallen
for a few shadows
in my day, but the
crafty cat always
gets his moth.

Always keep a clean litter box.
Cats are very fastidious. If your cat
wets outside the box or sprays a lot,
then the cat is probably sick.

cat
tips

february 25

Elizabeth Taylor once gave a Siamese cat
named Marcus as a gift to James Dean.

cat
trivia

Famous feline heroine, Scarlett,
rescued all five of her kittens from a
burning building in New York in 1996.

cat•e•va•sion

[kat-ee-vay-zhun] n.

maneuver enacted when
a cat's human calls.

 cat vocabulary

I have studied many
philosophers and many cats.
The wisdom of cats is
infinitely superior.

—Hippolyte Taine

The canary is safe.
Don't ask me about
the goldfish.

I don't know what happened. I was drinking coffee and plugging in the toaster and zap.

The Master's Cat was a kitten of Charles Dickens' favorite cat, Williamina, and the only kitten of the litter he kept. It is said he would snuff Dickens' reading candle to get attention.

cat
trivia

President Rutherford B. Hayes received
a Siamese cat from the American Consul
in Bangkok. The cat, Siam, was the first
Siamese cat to arrive in the United States.

To be a kitten is to be young at heart,
alert in mind, and carefree in spirit.

november 16

You are getting sleepy.
Your eyelids are
getting heavy. You want
to give me a big can of tuna.

march 1

Civilization is defined
by the presence of cats.

—Unknown

There is no snooze button
on a cat who wants breakfast.

—Unknown

march 2

I certainly know
my name. It's you
I don't acknowledge.

cat•a•pult
[ka-te-pult] n.
the sound a cat makes when trying
to eject a particularly bad hair ball

 cat vocabulary

march 3

Micetto was a grayish-red kitten
with black stripes born in the Vatican.
Micetto lived among Pope Leo XII's robes.

In Egyptian mythology the sun god
Ra took the form of a cat every night
to fight the evil serpent Apopis.
Solar eclipses marked the occasions
when Ra was defeated by Apopis.

cat
trivia

march 4

1. Cat around
2. Let the cat out of the bag
3. Raining cats and dogs
4. Catty
5. Cat and mouse game
6. Cat burglar
7. Catcall
8. Cat eye
9. Catfight
10. Catnap

top 10

Meow!

Cat Expressions

Surely you don't
think it was me?
Did you check the
puppy's alibi?

Tell me the truth.
Does this hairdo make me look fat?

What position does the poodle
play on the baseball team?

(Dog catcher.)

march 6

The prophet Mohammed was a renowned
cat lover. Legend has it that once,
when Mohammed was called to prayer,
he cut off the sleeve of his robe
rather than disturb his cat, Muezza,
who was sleeping on it.

cat
trivia

Cat hearing ranks among the top
in the animal kingdom. Cats can
hear sounds as high-pitched as 65 kHz;
human hearing stops at just 20 kHz.

cat
trivia

To Kill a Mockingbird
by Harper Cat Lee

 if cats could write

Hard day.

Hair ball.

'Nuff said.

march 8

If you yell at a cat, you're the one
who is making a fool of yourself.

—Unknown

If God created man in his own image,
you've got to wonder; in whose image
did he create the nobler cat?

—Unknown

The mighty hunter coils and springs!
Another ball of yarn bites the dust.

The Pet Crossing
by Cormac McCathy

if cats could write

march 10

Winston Churchill, a noted cat lover,
was quite fond of his kitten, Jock.
The kitten stayed by Churchill's side in bed
toward the end of Churchill's life.
Jock was mentioned in the Prime Minister's will.

november 6

Before Charles Lindbergh's transatlantic flight,
a photograph was taken of Lindbergh in
the cockpit with a kitten named Patsy.

march 11

And folks think
cats are stubborn?

(The man at our house
bought a dog whistle, and
the dog won't use it.)

So then she says to me,
"Why don't we try something different today."

All the civilized nap.

1. Balls
2. Yarn
3. Newspaper
4. Crinklies and shakies
5. Feathers
6. Catnip
7. Pom-poms
8. Curtains
9. Fingers and toes
10. Mice

top 10

cat toys

The Woods family left their cat, Sugar,
with new owners when they moved away,
but Sugar tracked the family
1,500 miles to their new home.

cat
trivia

november 3

Unsinkable Sam is the most famous British Naval mascot in history. He was rescued from three different ships when they sank.

march 14

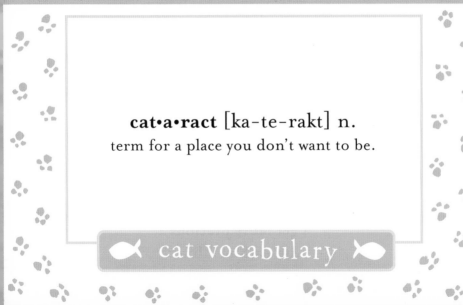

cat•a•ract [ka-te-rakt] n.
term for a place you don't want to be.

cat vocabulary

I get more precious
with each new life.

Pretend to give your cat fresh food.
If there is still food in the bowl and you
don't want to waste it, then shake it around
and your cat will think it is fresh.

cat
tips

november 1

We should be careful to get out of an experience
only the wisdom that is in it and stop there,
lest we be like the cat that sits down on a hot
stove-lid. She will never sit down on a hot
stove-lid again, and that is well; but also she
will never sit down on a cold one anymore.

—Mark Twain

Some furballs really
take it out of you.

Boo!

march 17

Tarawood Antigone is a brown
Burmese cat who holds the record for most
kittens in one litter. She had 19 kittens.

cat
trivia

october 30

Blackie holds the record
of richest cat in the world.
Ben Rea left his cat
£15 million in his will.

cat
trivia

Who are you calling a masked man?
This is my face.

I'm going to take a little nap. Wake me if you've got something interesting to say.

Who says only bad
things come in threes?

october 28

Beware of those
who dislike cats.

march 20

As Emily Brontë wrote *Wuthering Heights*,
her cat, Tiger, played at her feet.

Caroline Kennedy's famous childhood pet,
Tom Kitten, was given an obituary notice
by the press when he passed on in 1962.

cat
trivia

Aries

Some juicy news will reach you soon.
You'll want to tell others as soon as you can, but make
sure of all your facts before you do. Salacious details about
dogs don't mean much on face value to you, but they might
to your friends. Also, personal grooming will be a factor
in whether you get that promotion you've been seeking.

october 26

It isn't the size of
the cat, it's the size of
the love in the cat.

Every life should
have nine cats.

—Anonymous

Curiosity killed the cat,
Satisfaction brought it back!

—English proverb

I think you should lighten up.
Nothing's a toy in your eyes.

Scorpio

Sharpen your claws, Scorpio, as potential trouble looms
in your immediate future. Keep in mind that you reap what
you sow. The puppy you terrorize now will grow and grow.
The small children who make a wide circle around you
now will get water guns for the holidays. On the other paw,
excitement will mount when some new equipment
comes into your possession later in the month.

*kitty * horoscope*

march 24

President Calvin Coolidge was so fond of his cat,
Tiger, he walked around the White House
with the cat draped around his neck.
When Tiger got lost, Coolidge went on
the radio to ask for help finding him.

cat
trivia

Though cats don't always land
on their feet, they do have the
ability to "parachute" to safety
by spreading their legs and
arching their backs.

cat
trivia

cat•e•rad•i•ca•tion
[kat-ee-ra-de-kay-shun] n.
describes a cat while prowling; merciless.

 cat vocabulary

Hey, what do you
say we go mess
with the dog?

march 26

Cater to my every whim and
we'll get along famously.

A cat sleeps fat,
yet walks thin.

—Unknown

march 27

When the third Earl of Southhampton was put in the tower of London, his cat, Trixie, allegedly found and stayed with him for the next two years.

october 20

Andy, Florida Senator
Ken Myer's cat, fell from
the 16th floor of an apartment
building, setting a record for the
longest non-fatal fall by a cat.

cat
trivia

march 28

French novelist Colette was a firm cat-lover.
When she was in the U.S. she saw a cat sitting
in the street. She went over to talk to it and
the two of them mewed at each other for
a friendly minute. Colette turned to
her companion and exclaimed,
"Enfin! Quelqu'un qui parle français."
(At last! Someone who speaks French!)

october 19

Find your place in the sun...then take a nap.

If you shamefully misuse a cat once
she will always maintain a dignified reserve
toward you afterward. You will never
get her full confidence again.

—Mark Twain

It's not easy
to be humble.

I purr, therefore I am.

—Anonymous

Comfort your pets during storms—
they are frightened, too.

march 31

For kittens, joy is for the asking
and smiles are for the giving.

Zeus, an Asian Leopard Cat/Domestic Shorthair mix, is the world's most expensive cat. Zeus has an asking price of £100,000.

Always turn and look when your cat gazes
behind you with that intent look
in her eyes. Someday there might
actually be something there.

—Anonymous

Go ahead.
Resist this face.

Mrs. Johnson owns us both, so yeah,
I guess that means we're related.

In October not even a cat
is to be found in London.

—Anonymous

april 3

Timmy, another of President Coolidge's cats,
would allow the president's canary to
sleep between his paws.

Black cat superstitions began in America.
In both Asia and England, black
cats are considered lucky.

april 4

1. Napping in the morning sun

2. Napping at Disney World

3. Napping at the White House

4. Napping in the closet

5. Napping in the Rocky Mountains

6. Napping at the beach

7. Napping on Broadway

8. Napping in the afternoon sun

9. Napping on a cruise

10. Stretching after a good nap

top 10

cat vacations

To be a fool at the right
time is also an art.

—Swiss proverb

Oedipuss Rex
by Socatees

if cats could write

Did you hear about
the dog who found
a frog in his soup?

(The fly was on vacation.)

april 6

Be poised.

october 10

cat•e•gor•y
[ka-te-gor-ee] n.
rating for extreme
violence in cat movies

  cat vocabulary

Charles Dickens' favorite cat,
Williamina, was called William
until she had kittens.

Cats can jump seven
times their own height.

A home without a cat, and a well-fed,
well-petted and properly revered cat,
may be a perfect home, perhaps;
but how can it prove its title?

—Mark Twain

Someone say,
"Here, kitty, kitty."
I need a scratch.

april 9

How beautiful
it is to do nothing,
and then rest afterward.

—Spanish proverb

A lame cat is better
than a swift horse when
rats infest the palace.

—proverb

The title of Oldest Feline Mother goes to Kitty, who gave birth to two kittens at the age of 30. Kitty gave birth to a total of 218 kittens in her lifetime.

cat
trivia

october 6

Cats can be either
right-pawed or left-pawed.

cat
trivia

What's a cat's #1 excuse?

(The dog did it.)

I can't believe we have the same mother.

cat·as·tro·phe
[ke-tas-tre-fe] n.
French cat-derived word for asteroid.

 cat vocabulary

october 4

1. Inky
2. Midnight
3. Shadow
4. Boo
5. Catzilla
6. Blackie
7. Ashes
8. Ebony
9. Harley
10. Batsy

top 10

black cat names

I'll hide out here
until they put the
two-year-old to bed.

Beowulf,
a cat's worst nightmare

if cats could write

A cat named Hamlet escaped from his
carrier while on a flight out of Toronto.
He was found seven weeks later after
traveling about 373,000 miles.

cat
trivia

october 2

Though widely disputed,
an English cat by the name
Puss is claimed to be the
oldest cat ever at the age of
36 when she passed away.

cat
trivia

Speak to your cat.
Cats may not want a lot of attention,
but they like to be recognized.

cat
tips

october 1

Patience is but one
of my many virtues.

To err...just isn't feline.

A kitten is nobody's fool,
but everyone's best friend.

After an earthquake in Taiwan in December 1999,
an amazing cat was found still alive in
a collapsed building after 80 days.

cat
trivia

Famed mathematician Sir Isaac Newton,
who first described gravity, also invented the
swinging cat door to accommodate his many cats.

cat
trivia

So I turned like this
and I said to that cop,
"Do I look like a
40-pound tabby?"

Easter Bunny nothing!
What the world needs is an Easter Kitty.

What do you mean you
don't have the money?

The man who carries a cat
by the tail learns something that
can be learned in no other way.

—Mark Twain

Taurus

Taurus, life will get a lot easier for you and your owner when you accept your new lodgings and stop wandering back to your old house. Sure, you find yourself the center of attention and you get to tell your story and tell it well, but that is three highways you have to cross and, assuming you make it each time, there may come a time when your owner doesn't come after you. Be smart! Stay home!

cat•en•vy

[kat-en-vee] n.

perturbed state that exists
when Fido is getting attention.

 cat vocabulary

april 21

At 689 cats, Jack & Donna Wright of
Kingston, Ontario hold the record for
owning the largest number of cats.

cat
trivia

september 25

During the thirteenth century,
an Egyptian sultan left his entire
fortune to the needy cats of Cairo.
For years homeless cats received a free
daily meal courtesy of the late sultan.

cat
trivia

april 22

If stretching were wealth,
the cat would be rich.

—Unknown

It has been the providence
of Nature to give this creature
nine lives instead of one.

—Pilpay

april 23

I said NO PICTURES!

Libra

Romantic issues are about to take a turn for the better. Perhaps you can't see past the mangy coat of the alley cat on the back fence or drown out his off-key renditions of Sinatra's best love ballads. Worry no more, dear friend, as a new homeowner will adopt said cat and clean up his act. Do some fiscal housecleaning as well. High-interest debt can bring anyone down.

The oldest recorded living cat
in the world is Kataleena Lady.
The Burmese cat was born on March 11, 1977
and was 25 years old as of April 2002.

cat
trivia

Alexander Dumas, the author of
The Three Musketeers, had a cat named Mysouff.
Mysouff could predict what time his master
would finish work, regardless of how late
Dumas would work on a given night.

cat
trivia

cat·ef·fu·sion

[kat-i-fyu-zhun] n.

describes a cat during bathtime.

 cat vocabulary

There are a few
mysteries in life—
like what people
see in dogs.

My husband said it was him or the cat...
I miss him sometimes.

—Unknown

Most cats will come to
a whistle just like a dog.

cat
tips

But if you have me declawed, I won't be able to do this anymore!

Kittens never take things too seriously—
they just get up, move on, and shift
their attention to something new.

april 28

Cats can't see under their noses. That's why they can't seem to find food morsels on the floor.

A cat's heart beats somewhere between
110 to 140 beats per minute. That's twice
as fast as a normal human heart.

cat
trivia

april 29

A kitten is a one-of-a-kind work of
art that's precious and priceless.

september 17

Sometimes I feel I'm a lion trapped in a cat's body.
But then that goes away and I just sleep the rest of the day.

You're definitely
picking the wrong
day to mess with me.

Every dog has his day—but the nights
are reserved for the cats.

—Unknown

may 1

A cat has 230 bones in its body.
People only have 206.

Pulcinella, Italian composer Domenico Scarlatti's cat, used to leap onto the keyboard of the composer's harpsichord and walk up and down on the keys. Scarlatti appeased his cat by composing a fugue, which became known as "The Cat's Fugue."

Some people own cats and go
on to lead normal lives.

—Unknown

The plan is to nap all day,
gather my strength,
and annoy my
humans all night!

may 3

1. Dog teaser
2. Mouse chaser
3. Lap warmer
4. Nose tickler
5. Nerves calmer

6. Bird stalker
7. Fly batter
8. Toe attacker
9. Paper shredder
10. Child pleaser

top 10 uses for a cat

september 13

cat•sup
[kats-up] n.
slang employed by hip
cats meaning "what's up?"
or "how are you doing?"

 cat vocabulary

may 4

To say I don't care
about you is just not true.
Some of my best
friends are humans.

Which city is
a dog's favorite?

(New Yorkie.)

Cats have four
rows of whiskers.

september 11

A kitten is more amusing
than half the people one
is obliged to live with.

—Lady Sydney Morgan

Of Mice and Kittens
by John Steincat

 if cats could write

september 10

Never doubt who's really
running this show.

And it better be
name-brand chow.
I'll have none of that low
price 'Kitty Near the Sea'
stuff this week.

september 9

Do you see that kitten chasing so prettily her
own tail? If you could look with her eyes,
you might see her surrounded with hundreds
of figures performing complex dramas,
with tragic and comic issues, long conversations,
many characters, many ups and downs of fate.

—Ralph Waldo Emerson

may 8

Cats can sprint about
thirty-one miles per hour.

september 8

A cat's ear can pivot 180 degrees.
Cats use their hearing a lot like radar.

It's really the cat's house—
we just pay the mortgage.

—Unknown

I'm not actually
this furry. I was
playing under your
dresser. These are
dust bunnies.

Why does a dog
chase his tail?

(He's trying to
make ends meet.)

Captain Catrageous
by Rudyard Catling

if cats could write

Sometimes it's just fine
to be all dressed up
with nowhere to go.

september 5

1. Garfield

2. Heathcliff

3. Morris (9 Lives)

4. Bill the Cat (Bloom County)

5. Stimpy ("Ren and Stimpy")

6. Tom ("Tom and Jerry")

7. Salem ("Sabrina the Teenage Witch")

8. Abby the Olympic Tabby ("The Simpsons")

9. Arlene (Garfield's girlfriend)

10. Henrietta Pussycat (Mr. Rogers)

top 10
celebrity cats

Cats see about six times better than people
do at night because of the *tapetum lucidum*, a layer
of reflective cells that absorb extra light.

cat
trivia

september 4

Cat brains are more
similar to human brains
than dog brains are.

CAT· scan
[kat-skan] n.
trance-like state acquired before
windows when searching for birds.

 cat vocabulary

Yeah, white may
be pretty, but what do
I do after labor day?

The world is a warm bowl
of fresh milk. Lap it up!

Dogs have owners,
cats have staff.

—Unknown

may 15

A cat's whiskers act as feelers,
helping the cat judge the
exact width of any passage.

A cat will spend almost a third
of its life grooming itself.

If you have to move to a new home, put some unwashed clothing in the room with the cat and keep the cat inside for at least three weeks or the cat might try to go to the old home.

Just a few minutes of playing
with your kitten will keep
you smiling all day long.

It is so biker-looking.
What kind of cat has
a Mohawk anyway?

God made the cat in order
to give man the pleasure
of caressing the tiger.

Let's get our stories straight. And remember,
eye contact is a presumption of guilt.

No heaven will not ever be heaven be;
Unless my cats are there to welcome me.

—Unknown

may 19

Cats will practically never meow at other cats.
They save meowing for humans.

august 28

Cats can't sweat;
they have no sweat glands.

cat
trivia

Cats invented
assertiveness training.

Do not sneak up
on me like that.

Gemini

It's clear that you like to help with various household chores from gift wrapping to balancing the checkbook. However, you need to be more attentive to the matter at hand. While it is tempting to chew on ribbon and bed down on important documents, you must learn the proper way to be a helper. Pay close attention to your human. You don't want information to disappear from your mind as soon as you hear it.

A cat is beautiful; it suggests
ideas of luxury, cleanliness,
voluptuous pleasures.

—Charles Baudelaire

Cats can't move
their jaws sideways.

Cats have excellent memory,
which can last as long as 16 hours.
Cat memory is better than the memories
of dogs, monkeys, and orangutans.

may 23

In Egypt, the cats…afford evidence that
animal nature is not altogether intractable,
but that when well-treated they are
good at remembering kindness.

—Aelian

Just thought you should know—every time you move the plant higher, it gets harder for me to eat it.

cat•es•o•ter•ic•a
[kat-e-se-ter-ik-a] n.
describes a cat when meowing

cat vocabulary

Virgo

The days are growing longer, dear Virgo. Winter will fall like a dark cloud over your sunny napping spot. This just might throw you into a panic—but don't fall into this trap. Phone a friend. Go to church. Knit something. Just hang in there: spring is right around the corner! Also, avoid the lottery and all other games of chance for the next few weeks.

Today's mice don't
even put up a fight.

august 22

A cat can climb down from a tree
without the assistance of the fire department
or any other agency. The proof is that no
one has ever seen a cat skeleton in a tree.

—Unknown

A cat's normal body
temperature is 101.5 degrees.

august 21

Cats make about 100
different vocal sounds.
By way of comparison,
dogs only make about 10.

All cats love a
cushioned couch.

—Theocritus

Pretty is as pretty does.

Just looking at me made
you yawn, didn't it?

I look good
from any angle.

A 15-year-old cat
has likely spent ten
years of its life asleep.

Studies show cats have a homing ability
that uses the cat's biological clock,
the angle of the sun over the horizon,
and, amazingly, the Earth's magnetic field.

I can say with sincerity that I like cats.
A cat is an animal which has more
human feelings than almost any other.

—Emily Brontë

After a long day
of lying on the sofa,
I like to unwind
by taking a nap.

Sit and watch a kitten for
an afternoon. In that short time,
you'll discover the joys of life.

In the car, face the carrier
so the cat can see you.

cat
tips

Ears. Scratch. Now.

A cat will never drown
if she sees the shore.

—Francis Bacon

june 2

A group of adult cats
is called a *clowder*.

Some cats have freckles.
They can appear anywhere on a
cat's skin and even in its mouth.

cat
trivia

june 3

1. A dirty litter box
2. A puppy
3. A child with a water gun
4. Vacuum cleaners
5. Climbing out of trees

6. Cheap cat food
7. Too much adoration
8. Being ignored
9. Slick floors
10. Free-range toddlers

top 10 cat pet peeves

In a cat's eyes,
all things belong to cats.

—English saying

Psst. Mouse. C'mere.
I've got something to show ya.

What do you
get if you cross a
dog with a daisy?

(A collie-flower.)

june 5

A group of kittens
is called a *kindle*.

When cats get bored they
show it through excessive
licking, chewing, or biting.

cat
trivia

june 6

The Caterberry Tail
by Geoffrey Chaucer

 if cats could write

A cat is a lion in a
jungle of small bushes.

—Indian proverb

A cat is an example of
sophistication minus civilization.

—Anonymous

cat and mouse
[kat and maus] adj.

a lopsided battle that
has been mischaracterized
as a classic struggle

 cat vocabulary

Tell me he isn't still staring at me.

I could endure anything
before but a cat, and
now he's a cat to me.

—William Shakespeare

All cats have blue eyes
when they're born.

Calico cats are
almost always female.

cat
trivia

I'm thinking the dog
next door is not very smart.

(He chases parked cars.)

This is torture.
Someone call the ASPCA.

june 11

Mission: Window Shade
Pull String.

Decision: Accepted.

1. Sleeping in the sunlight

2. Stretching

3. Chasing birds

4. Scratching furniture

5. Exploring

6. Avoiding hair balls

7. Bathing

8. Staring out the window

9. Pawing something around the room

10. Staying out of sight

top 10

cat pastimes

Ancient Egyptians believed that Bast
was the mother of all cats on Earth.
To the Egyptians, cats were sacred animals.

august 4

The same region of the brain is responsible for emotion in both cats and people.

cat·er·pil·lar
[ka-ter-pill-er] n.
used by cat husband or wife
when it becomes obvious
that the significant other has
snatched the favorite pillow

 cat vocabulary

I won't roll in that again.

My sister crying, our maid howling,
our cat wringing her hands.

—William Shakespeare

The Adventures of Tom–Cat Sawyer
by Mark Twine

if cats could write

I trust my dinner is ready
and waiting for me in
its usual spot.

Honest as a cat when
the cream is out of reach.

—Anonymous

june 16

Cats have pads on their front paws
that prevent them from sliding on
slippery surfaces when jumping.

july 31

A cat drinks by lapping liquid up
with the underside of its tongue,
not the top as one might suspect.

cat
trivia

You see the beauty of the world
Through eyes of unalloyed content,
And in my study chair upcurled,
Move me to pensive wonderment.

—Anonymous

Then you shouldn't have put
the dinner rolls in my basket.

How many dogs
does it take to screw
in a lightbulb?

(All of 'em. One to turn it,
and the rest to run around
in circles barking at it.)

july 29

Kittens don't worry about what
will happen in the future—they
enjoy every moment as it comes.

Cats have true fur,
which means that they
have both an undercoat
and an outercoat.

The phenomenon of cats tracing
their owners to a place they have never
been before is known as Psi-trailing.

june 20

Your veterinarian might
provide medication to help
your cat sleep on long trips.

cat
tips

A dog may be your friend, but a cat is your equal.

Yes, in fact,
I am the queen.

The cat has nine lives:
three for playing,
three for straying,
three for staying.

—English proverb

Cancer

Does something in your life not "add up"? Bills and family got you feeling overloaded? Don't worry, relief is on the way in the form of a good-looking Persian moving in next door. Unfortunately, another big change looms on your horizon in the form of an allergic child or unforgiving owner, and you might be spending much more of your time in the out-of-doors.

★ ★ ★ ★ ★ ★ ★ kitty ★ horoscope ★ ★ ★ ★ ★ ★ ★ ★ ★ ★

cat•el•e•gance
[kat-e-li-gen(t)s] n.
describes a cat while lounging

 cat vocabulary

june 23

Cats don't have a true collarbone
and can squeeze their bodies through
tight spaces, provided they can get
their heads through first.

cat
trivia

The cat is the only
domestic animal that isn't
mentioned in the Bible.

cat•e•go•cen•tri•cit•y
[kat-ee-go-sen-tri-se-tee] n.
a cat's perpetual state of being

 cat vocabulary

Leo

Get over yourself, Leo. You've gotten way too caught up in this King of the Jungle thing. Lions are cats but not all cats are lions, something you better keep in mind during neighborhood events involving other species. Some intriguing discussions could take place throughout the evening, but it would be wise NOT to contradict any bulldogs or play any games of Twister with pet pythons.

Then is it good luck
if I cross your path?

july 22

We're not finicky, just discriminating.
This fish doesn't smell fresh.

Cats step with both left legs,
then both right legs when
walking or running. The only other
animals that walk in such a manner
are the giraffe and the camel.

cat
trivia

Young cats can differentiate
two identical sounds that are
a mere 18 inches apart at a
distance of as much as 60 feet.

cat
trivia

What sort of philosophers are we,
who know absolutely nothing
of the origin and destiny of cats?

—Henry David Thoreau

If you really want
something, you just
have to get it yourself.

Cats use more than
500 muscles to leap,
jump, and sprint.

cat
trivia

Have at least a week's supply of pet food
on hand at all times. Store the dry food
in airtight/waterproof containers.

cat
tips

When a cat is alone
she never purrs.

—Samuel Johnson

What do you
mean shades of gray?
There is only one
gray in this world
worth having.
This gray.

june 30

Cats are the most common pets in
the U.S. There are approximately
66 million cats to 58 million dogs.

july 17

The cat is the only animal
that walks on its claws instead
of the pads of its feet.

july 1

A little drowsing cat is an
image of perfect beatitude.

—Jules Champfleury

If you want an honest
opinion of yourself,
ask your cat.

Oh, sure ... I think the puppy's just to die for.

They say the test of
literary power is whether a
man can write an inscription.
I say, "Can he name a kitten?"

—Samuel Butler

july 3

It is not safe to pick
a kitten up by its neck.
Only a cat can do it safely.

cat
trivia

july 14

The cat family is one of the
oldest mammalian families,
having split from other mammals
at least 40 million years ago.

cat
trivia

july 4

1. Always land on your feet.

2. You can never take too many naps.

3. A spit bath is better than no bath at all.

4. The higher you climb, the more perspective you get.

5. Sometimes it is better not to run with the crowd.

6. No matter how much you paid for that couch, sharp things will destroy it.

7. Tuna is overrated.

8. Keep your bathroom clean.

9. Sing loud, even if you can't sing well.

10. Sometimes dogs will chase you.

top 10 cat proverbs

There is no shame in not knowing...
the shame lies in not finding out.

—Russian proverb

The Taming of the Shrew
by William Shakesclaw

 if cats could write

cat•a•comb
[kat-a-cohm] n.
what you should use to keep
cats from getting hairballs

 cat vocabulary

So then she gets out this blow-dryer…

What happened
when Fido attended
the flea circus?

(He stole the show.)

july 7

Newborn kittens' ear
canals don't begin to
open for nine days.

july 10

The ancestor of all domestic cats is the
African Wild Cat, which still exists today.

Ah! Cats are a mysterious kind of folk.
There is more passing in their
minds than we are aware of.

—Sir Walter Scott

july 9

When the mouse laughs at the cat,
there is a hole nearby.

—Nigerian proverb